LUNA LITTLE LEGS

This sensitively written storybook has been created to help very young children understand about domestic abuse and coercive control.

Luna loves playing with her friends at kitten club, but at home things are different. One terrible night, Luna overhears a domestic abuse incident and, when her own name is mentioned, she wonders if it might be her fault. Accompanied by beautiful and engaging illustrations, the story provides a vehicle for talking with children about their experiences, safety and emotional wellbeing.

Three potential endings allow the story to be personalised to the individual child:

- In ending 1, Luna is comforted by her Mummy and remains at home
- In ending 2, Luna and her Mummy move to a refuge, and eventually into their own home
- In ending 3, Luna's Daddy apologises for his behaviour promising to change, and she and her Mummy move back into the family home.

Through age-appropriate rhyming language, this story explores children's common reactions to domestic abuse, shows them that they are not alone and helps them talk about their feelings. It is an essential tool for all early years practitioners, as well as professionals working with children and families who are experiencing, or have experienced, domestic abuse and coercive control.

Catherine Lawler is a qualified specialist children's counsellor, trauma practitioner and a childhood survivor of domestic abuse. She has extensive experience of working with children, young people and families as well as developing and facilitating training on the issue of domestic abuse and coercive control. Catherine is co-author of *Domestic Violence and Children: A Handbook for Schools and Early Years* (Routledge, 2010) and *Floss and the Boss: Helping Children Learn About Domestic Abuse and Coercive Control* (Routledge, 2021).

Norma Howes has trained in social work, child forensic psychology and psychotherapy. She is also a trainer and consultant for workers from agencies about the impact of all forms of trauma, abuse and neglect. She has a special interest in domestic abuse and sexual trauma. She has written Guides for Community Care Inform: A Trauma model for working with i) domestic abuse, ii) sexual exploitation, iii) contact between children and their families and a Guide on the Neurobiological Impact of Contact.

Nicky Armstrong, BA(Hons) Theatre Design, MA Slade School of Fine Arts, has illustrated 30 books which have been translated and published in seven countries. She has achieved major commissions in both mural and fine art painting.

Luna Little Legs

Helping Young Children to Understand Domestic Abuse and Coercive Control

Catherine Lawler and Norma Howes

Illustrated by Nicky Armstrong

Routledge
Taylor & Francis Group

LONDON AND NEW YORK

Cover image: Nicky Armstrong

First published 2022
by Routledge
4 Park Square, Milton Park, Abingdon, Oxon OX14 4RN

and by Routledge
605 Third Avenue, New York, NY 10158

Routledge is an imprint of the Taylor & Francis Group, an informa business

British Library Cataloguing-in-Publication Data
A catalogue record for this book is available from the British Library

Library of Congress Cataloging-in-Publication Data
A catalog record has been requested for this book

ISBN: 978-1-032-07259-3 (pbk)
ISBN: 978-1-003-20618-7 (ebk)

DOI: 10.4324/9781003206187

Typeset in Bembo
by Apex CoVantage, LLC

This book is dedicated to my beautiful cat Isobel, the real Luna. She is my constant companion and source of unconditional love. I had heard that many people become cat mums or dads more through accident than design and this was the case for me. The day Isobel rocked up to my house and refused to leave was a blessed day. She turned up out of the blue at a time in my life when I would soon desperately need her, I didn't know this, but she clearly did.

This book is also dedicated to the little people out there who live with the terror of domestic abuse, who attempt to navigate this every day and are finally seen as victims in their own right.

Catherine

ABOUT THE ENDINGS – WHY THREE ALTERNATIVES WITH NO FINITE ENDING?

We wondered when writing this book how to end Little Luna's story. Every child's lived experience will be unique and that's the reason we want you to choose how to end the book in a way that will fit with the actual or possible ending(s) of the child you are supporting. This will enable individual children to connect Little Luna's experiences with their own and, like her, be able to better understand and have words for their own feelings, confusions, losses and gains. And, indeed, hopes for the future.

Three potential endings allow the story to be personalised to the individual child:

- **In ending 1**, Luna is comforted by her Mummy and remains at home.
- **In ending 2**, Luna and her Mummy move to a refuge, and eventually into their own home.
- **In ending 3**, Luna's Daddy apologises for his behaviour and promises to change, and she and her Mummy move back into the family home.

Within the story book, 'The End' will appear after each section, and continuing onto the next section will be dependent on the lived experience of the child you are supporting. When finishing a section, professionals should take the opportunity to explore and reflect on the story with the child using care, good judgement and creativity. The storybook can be a gateway to introducing other activities and resources helpful to children.

If you consider the book would be useful to read with or use with an older child it may be useful to share all three endings. We have used it with young teenagers who are able to reflect on the choices their parents made or didn't make. They were asked for their views about the usefulness of the book for young children and in doing that looked at the book with the eyes of the very young child they were when Luna's experiences were theirs and as the adolescents they are now opening up discussions about their expectations of the behaviour of their current and future partners.

Once upon a time not so long ago

Lived a kitten named Luna Little Legs

she has come to say 'hello'.

Luna's furry friends are Cookie, Ringo, and Mittens.

They go to cat club every day to play with other kittens.

Cat club is fun where kittens scoot around,

With lots of toys to play with and a big playground.

There is story time and snacks and lots of little beds

Where kittens who need to nap, can rest their sleepy heads.

At home Luna mews for milk, she purrs and gobbles her tea.

Her four little paws pad up and down

and she starts to feel sleepy.

Her two little eyes start to close, her head bobs to and fro

And Mummy sings a lullaby singing off to sleep you go.

Then once upon a terrible time

Luna little legs did not feel fine.

She had wobbly feelings in her legs and her tummy

They happened when Daddy was scratchy with Mummy.

When Daddy scratched Mummy, he would hiss and bite.

Poor Luna's fur would go stiff with fright.

Her little legs would shake, and her tummy would splat

Poor little Luna was a very scared cat.

One terrible night when she was in bed,

Little Luna's heart filled up with dread.

She heard angry shouting and heard her name

Was it something she did? Could she be to blame?

Mummy came in to see her that night

She kissed Luna's nose and hugged her tight.

"No, no, no Little Luna you're not to blame

Never, never, ever even if you hear your name.

I can see you are shaky, and you feel so sad,

But it's not your fault and you are not bad,"

"If you feel shaky at home or when we are apart

Look at your little legs and there see your heart.

When you see your heart remember this

Mummy's sending a big warm kiss.

Catch my kiss in your paw and know

I love you more and more".

At home sometimes Luna felt happy, sometimes she felt sad.

Sometimes she felt angry, sometimes she felt glad.

She tried hard to remember what Mummy had said

It helped when Mummy cuddled her and

stroked her little head.

The End, Part 1

Then one night there was a shout like a big clap of thunder.

Blanket, table quick Luna went under.

Mummy said, "Quick, quick Little Luna we have to rush."

They ran out of the house and hid under a bush.

They waited a while and the moon shone so bright.

But they knew they couldn't stay there all through the night.

They could not go home, it was not safe.

Mummy said, "We're going to live in a different place."

"There's a place called a Refuge that's where we will go."

"What's that?" asked Luna, she wanted to know.

"It's for Mummies and kittens not for scratchy cats,

It's where we will sleep and we can relax."

The Refuge felt strange, lots of new cats to meet.

New games to play and new food to eat.

But no Cookie or Ringo and not even Mittens.

Her toys left at home, she can't share with new kittens.

Sometimes Little Luna felt sad but mostly so glad.

With no shouts or scratches to make her feel bad.

She soon settled into this different new place

Until Mummy found a new home to live in always.

This new home Mummy found they moved into quite soon,

With enough space for them and a little spare room

For visits from Cookie, Ringo and Mittens

And spend time with new friends, grownup cats and kittens.

The End, Part 2

But Daddy said he was sorry, and

promised he would be kind.

He remembered scratchy shouts hurt Little Luna's mind.

He promised to change and not have all his own way.

He promised Mummy and Luna could have fun and play.

So, Mummy said "Yes, we will give it a try

But if Daddy is scratchy or scary, we will say goodbye."

For Mummy knew Little Luna needed kisses and smiles

Not just for sometimes but for all the whiles.